SPACE MONSTERS
OF THE OLD WEST

**NOE TORRES &
JOHN LEMAY**

**BICEP BOOKS
ROSWELL, NEW MEXICO**

An *Original* Publication of BICEP BOOKS

Copyright © 2020 by Bicep Books

All rights reserved. No portion of this book may be reproduced in any form without permission from the publisher, except as permitted by U.S. copyright law.

First Bicep Books printing October 2020

Printed in the USA

For Daniel Cohen, who wrote books like these that fired the imaginations of many young readers interested in the paranormal.

CONTENTS

Introduction...7

Chapter 1
The Mummy from Mars...9

Chapter 2
The Blob from Outer Space...17

Chapter 3
Pascagoula's Space Ghouls...25

Chapter 4
Bigfoot from the Moon...29

Chapter 5
The Crawfordsville Monster...37

Chapter 6
Attack of the Water Babies...45

Chapter 7
Flying Mechanical Serpent...51

Chapter 8
Spring-Heeled Jack Comes to America...59

Chapter 9
Old West Chupacabras...67

Chapter 10
The Flying Turtle UFO Monster...75

**Chapter 11
The Invisible
Aerolite Monster...79
Chapter 12
The Alien
Submarine Monster...83
Chapter 13
Aliens with
Bows and Arrows?...93
Chapter 14
Dinosaurs from Outer
Space!...99
Chapter 15
The Alien's Grave...105**

About the Authors...118

INTRODUCTION

When you first saw this book, you might have thought that it was fiction, but it's not. Though this may seem hard to believe, all the stories in this book came from real newspaper articles published during the era of the Old West.

The Old West period took place between 1865-1895, beginning right after the Civil War ended and lasting all the way to the end of the 1800s. These were the days of cowboys and outlaws like Billy the Kid and Jesse James. Cars hadn't been invented yet and so people traveled on horses and carriages. Messages were sent over telegrams rather than cell phones. Obviously, the Old West was a long ways off from the technology we have today. One thing the Old West for sure didn't have was airplanes. The closest thing to airplanes back then were hot air balloons.

So, when cowboys and pioneers saw strange things flying in the sky back then, they could only be a UFO. Technically anything that you see in the sky but can't identify is an unidentified flying object to you until you learn what it was. But, since airplanes were still an invention of the future, most of what people in the 1800s saw streak through the air could have very likely have been spacecraft from other worlds or dimensions.

And people back then didn't just see possible spacecraft, they also sometimes saw the pilots. Some looked like humans, but many others could be described as aliens, and a few others could only be called space monsters.

And as you can tell from the title, this book's focus will be on the stranger, more monstrous alien life-forms recorded in the old pioneer newspaper articles.

As you read this book, you can decide for yourself whether these articles were simply a bored reporter's joke on readers, or if maybe, just maybe, they were describing real visitors that weren't of this earth...

CHAPTER 1
THE MUMMY FROM MARS

Imagine that while digging in the dirt outside you find a strange object in the ground. It looks like a huge rock, except for that it is smooth and shaped like an egg. You crack it open and find out that it isn't a rock after all. Because, inside you find a metallic jar. And within the jar is the strangest thing of all: a tiny mummified body. It looks human except for that it has something growing out of its forehead that looks like an elephant's trunk!

Well, according to a French newspaper article published on June 17, 1864, this is exactly what happened to two American archeologists named Paxton and Davis.

Specifically, the French paper claimed they had received a letter from Richmond, Virginia, telling of the strange tale. It stated that the two geologists were exploring the area around James Peak, Colorado, when they found a huge meteorite that had lain there 'for millions of years.'

For six days, the geologists and their team dug around the huge meteorite. Eventually, they found a hollow chamber within the space rock, and within that they found a metal vase with hieroglyphic writing on it. Hieroglyphic writing refers to strange symbols used in the writings of ancient cultures like the Egyptians. It's also a common staple of UFO crash lore, since crash debris found in the 1947 Roswell Incident also had hieroglyphic writing on it.

It took the geologists three days to carefully pry the lid off of the vase. That's where they found a strange coffin so old that stalagmites were growing on it. Inside was the calcified body of a human-like being only four feet tall. Coincidentally, this is also the height given to many aliens supposedly seen today.

In addition to the strange trunk growing from its forehead, it also had extra-long arms. And though it had five fingers on each hand like a human, the fourth finger was much shorter than the rest.

With the body was found a silver plaque that all but confirmed it was an alien, or an "interplanetary voyager" as the paper called it. On the plaque was drawings of the sun and the planets, with Mars emphasized above all the others. This led the newspapers to title the strange story "An Inhabitant of the Planet Mars."

At first glance, this all seems very encouraging. After all, the size of the alien body and the strange alien writing all sound very similar to the Roswell Incident, which hadn't even happened yet.

But, as it turned out, the story was a hoax. It was concocted by a young reporter named Henri de Parville, the penname of Francois Henri Peudefer (1838-1909).

Hendri De Parville.

SPACE MONSTERS OF THE OLD WEST

The story was still far from over, though. Parville adapted his fake article into an entire book! It was called *An Inhabitant of the Planet Mars*.

A few years later the story resurfaced again in the form of a copycat article. A reporter in South America had either read Parville's book or his article and made their own version of the story.

The article was published on October 13, 1877 in *La Capital*, a newspaper from Argentina. Even the names of the geologists were reused! However, this time they found the strange rock, and the alien body inside of it, along the Carcarana River in South America.

There's no need to go into further details, since they are exactly the same. In the 1970s, UFO researchers saw this article. Because they were unaware that it was simply a copy of an earlier hoax, they sent two expeditions to South America to explore the area where the alien was found. Naturally, nothing turned up, and eventually Ufologists discovered the earlier article from which the story descended.

MUMMIFIED PYGMY FOUND

LUSK, Wyo.—(U.P)—A mummified pygmy, believed by scientists to be a progenitor of the present human race, was exhibited in Lusk recently. The mummy is owned by Homer F. Sherrill, of Crawford, Neb., and has baffled scientists in various parts of the country where it has been sent for classification. It was unearthed in a cave on a slope of one of the Peaks of Pedro mountain, near Casper, Wyo.

Article about the 1932 San Pedro Mummy.

SPACE MONSTERS OF THE OLD WEST

And yet, our story still isn't over. As the old saying goes, sometimes truth is stranger than fiction. In the 1930s, a tiny mummified, alien-like body was found. This was no hoax, as the body was seen by many people.

In 1932, two prospectors mining for gold dynamited a cave in the San Pedro Mountains of Wyoming. When the dust settled, they found they had uncovered a small four foot by four-foot room. Inside of the room they found a small six-inch mummy with a very strange shaped head. A head that many people would compare to an alien's, except, back in the 1930s, the Roswell-type aliens were not a part of popular culture.

Because of that, the mummy was instead compared to the mythical "little people" of Native American legend. And where is this mummy today? Can't we test its DNA to prove what it is? Well, we could but sadly the mummy disappeared back in 1975. And, unless the body is found, we may never know what it was.

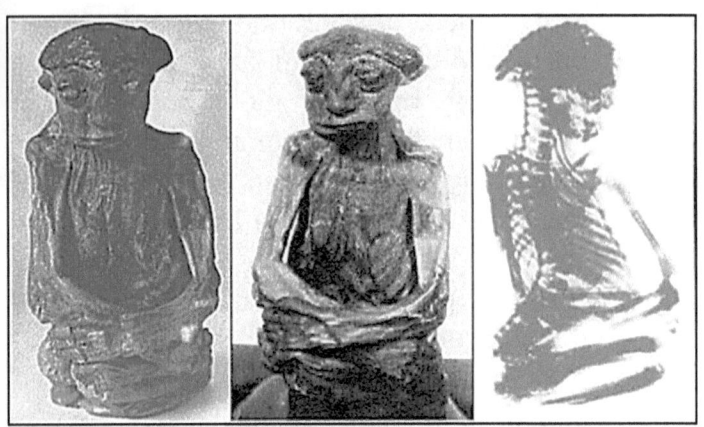

The 1932 San Pedro Mummy.

CHAPTER 2
THE BLOB FROM OUTER SPACE

In 1958, one of the most popular space monster movies of all time was released: *The Blob*. In the film, a meteor crashes on Earth and hatches a glob of red, creeping goo that consumes everyone in its path. What most people don't know is that *The Blob* was partially inspired by a real event!

Eight years before the movie was released, on September 26, 1950, in Pennsylvania, two police officers, John Collins and Joe Keenan, were on patrol when suddenly, a strange purple object floated across the beam of their headlights. They watched in amazement as the strange purple object landed in a field. Naturally, they went to the landing site to investigate. There they found a purple domed disk composed of a quivering space jelly that measured six feet in diameter! At its highest point, the dome was one foot thick. When they turned off their flashlights, the two policemen were shocked to see that the object glowed with a strange mist! Odder still, the men felt that the strange substance was somehow alive. Not sure how to handle this odd, potentially harmful substance, they radioed for backup. They were soon joined by Sergeant Joe Cook and Patrolman James Cooper.

When the lawmen tried to pick up samples of the giant, Jell-O-like object, it began to fall apart. The bits that stuck to their hands began to evaporate. Thirty minutes later, the entire substance had disappeared.

Not as exciting as the movie *The Blob*, but strange just the same. However, space jelly had been falling from the skies since the 1500s, and in the 1800s people called it "star rot."

SPACE MONSTERS OF THE OLD WEST

"Star rot" was a very strange see-through substance that was often found on the ground after meteor showers occurred. One of the best documented cases of "star rot" occurred in Amherst, Massachusetts on August 13, 1819. That night, between 8 and 9 p.m., a bright ball of white light resembling "burnished silver" crashed into the ground. Actually, crash may not be the right word, and it may not have been an ordinary meteor.

The reason we say that is because one of the witnesses claimed that the ball of light came down slowly—or at least much slower than the typical meteor or shooting star usually did.

The object fell near the home of a man named Erastus Dewey. The next morning he walked out his front door to find a mass of strange goo twenty feet away in his yard. Eventually, a scientist named Professor Rufus Graves found out about it and came to investigate. Like any good researcher, he interviewed the witnesses and took samples of the strange goo.

Amherst College, circa 1903.

SPACE MONSTERS OF THE OLD WEST

Graves's description of the goo was very similar to what the two Pennsylvania patrolmen saw in 1950. Graves said that it looked like a saucer or plate lying face down on the ground. In other words, it was shaped like a circle. He said that it was "of a bright buff color." He said that it was covered in a film that protected it from the air. When he pulled off the thin lining, he said that it smelt so bad that it made him dizzy. Creepier still, he said a few moments after he pulled off the lining that the blob turned red, like blood.

This is interesting because this is very similar to the movie *The Blob*. At first the blob is clear until it attacks its first victim. After that, the blob turns red from the blood.

You might now be wondering if this story was a hoax inspired by *The Blob*. People will, after all, sometimes make up stories set many years in the past. But that's not what this is. The story of Rufus Graves and the mysterious red, star rot was published in scientific journals of the time. So it's no hoax.

Portrayal of Professor Rufus Graves by an Actor in a Stage Play (Amherst College Archives).

After a few days, the sample that Graves collected began to evaporate into the air. Eventually all that was left was a dark residue within the container that once held the alien mass.

But the strangeness doesn't end there. Meteor falls should be totally random, and yet, several years later another strange objet fell from the stars near the same spot. It left behind the same strange residue.

Then, in October of 1864, another object crashed down in Hubbardston, Massachusetts, which is about 40 miles from Amherst, where the "blob" of 1819 touched down.

A newspaper called the *Worcester Spy* reported on how a "large meteor" fell near the shore of Parker's Pond. Like Rufus Graves did 40 years earlier, an investigator the next morning went to the impact sight and found "a mass...of a gelatinous, light colored, semi-transparent substance, described by some parties to be as large as a hogshead."

Unfortunately, the mass evaporated rather quickly, leaving nothing behind for us to study today...

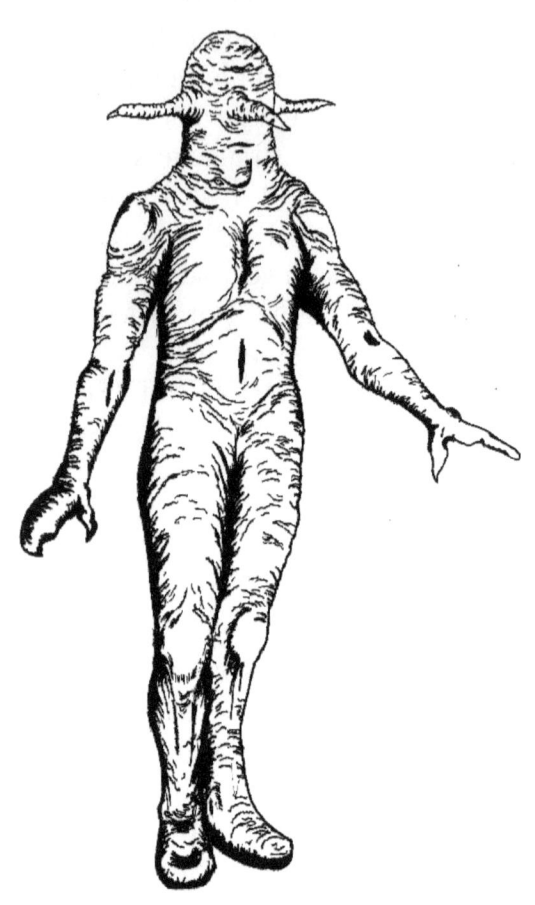

Pascagoula Alien by Neil Riebe.

CHAPTER 3
PACAGOULA'S SPACE GHOULS

On October 11, 1973, Calvin Parker and Charles Hickson were out fishing on the Pascagoula River in Mississippi. Hickson was sitting on the pier and had just gotten a fish hooked on his line when he heard a strange whirring noise behind him. He turned to look and saw a strange craft pulsating with blue light. It hovered about a foot off the ground.

Hickson and Parker both became paralyzed as they observed the UFO. A door opened on the craft and out of it floated three strange beings. They were truly alien in appearance, with wrinkly skin like an elephant's. They had no eyes or ears, and had strange protrusions sticking out of their head.

Parker and Hickson remember floating into the craft and being examined by the strange beings. They didn't know how much time had passed, but sometime later, they suddenly found themselves outside, standing on the shore of the Pascagoula River.

The men called the sheriff's department to tell of their strange encounter. The story got leaked to the press, and soon the two men were famous as UFO abductees. In fact, they are probably two of the most well-known abductees of the 1970s.

While the "Pascagoula Incident" is quite well known today, people might be shocked to learn that Pascagoula was visited by aliens 99 years earlier. Newspapers report that on August 13, 1874, a strange alien storm passed over Pascagoula.

That week, the residents of Pascagoula had endured abnormally high temperatures. As it turned out, it was the first in a series of odd events.

On the night of the 13th occurred an intense thunderstorm with hail and lightning. The storm was followed by what the paper called a "luminous electric cloud." Stranger yet, people said that the "cloud" made the air get extremely hot as it moved past them. One woman, who stuck her head out the window to watch the cloud, said that it felt like "her hair had been scorched from her head." It was so hot that she feared her house had caught fire.

An old man taking a nap outside was awakened from the cloud's intense heat. He watched as the cloud sailed over him and illuminated everything in its path. It was so hot that he said to his brother, "The world is on fire!"

These were just a few witnesses who saw the strange cloud, which many UFO experts today believe was a spacecraft. But, if that's the case, why didn't the people of the time call it a UFO?

The reason is simple, the terms UFO and flying saucer hadn't been invented yet. That's why the witnesses described the strange glowing object as a "luminous cloud."

And that's still not the strangest thing about this story. One of this book's authors, Noe Torres, is a Ufologist, or someone who studies UFOs. He interviewed Calvin Parker about his alien abduction in the 1970s. Torres also spoke to Parker about the UFO sighting in 1874. When he showed Parker the UFO's flight path he was shocked. He told Torres that the UFO in 1874 flew over the exact spot where he was abducted in 1973.

Perhaps the aliens from 1874 returned in 1973, almost 100 years later. Only this time they did more than just fly over the town...

CHAPTER 4
BIGFOOT FROM THE MOON

Bigfoot has always presented a challenge for researchers because, on the surface, Bigfoot appears to be a normal animal. Or, normal in the sense that despite its strange ape-like appearance, Bigfoot has no supernatural powers like a ghost or alien.

And yet, if Bigfoot really is just an undiscovered animal, why can't anyone capture one or at least find a dead body in the woods? Some researchers have put forth the idea that it's because Bigfoot is actually an alien not of this world.

Artist Jared Olive's rendition of the "Crazy Bear" sitting in its cave.

SPACE MONSTERS OF THE OLD WEST

Believe it or not, a story from the Old West actually supports this idea. Many Native American tribes across the United States had legends about hairy giants similar to Bigfoot. A tribe from Humboldt County, California, had a legend about the creatures. They called them "Crazy Bears" instead of Bigfoot, and claimed they were dropped off on Earth by visitors from above.

The story of the Crazy Bears was found in a journal written in 1888 by a cattleman named Mr. Wyatt. Wyatt had spent the winter with the tribe and was even learning to speak their language.

One day, while out in the woods, Wyatt came across a local tribesman carrying a platter of raw meat. Wondering what was going on, and who the meat was for, Wyatt began to question the man. Although reluctant at first, the tribesman finally allowed Wyatt to follow him to a nearby shallow cave along a cliff face.

Inside the mysterious cave, a very strange creature sat cross-legged on the ground. The being looked like a man, except that it was very large, muscular and hairy. The man-beast was entirely covered in long, shiny, black hair, except for its palms and an area around its eyes. Also, the creature seemed to have no neck, its head seeming to rest right on top of its shoulders.

Despite its frightening appearance, the monster did not seem aggressive or dangerous. As Wyatt and the other man approached, the creature sat peacefully, eating its meat. In fact, Wyatt said he even went back to visit the creature on several occasions. Unfortunately, Wyatt's diary gives no details of his other visits and does not say if he ever tried to communicate with the creature in any way.

Curious about the man-beast, Wyatt asked the tribesmen questions about their mysterious "guest." Finally, after trading one man two pounds of tobacco, an axe, and a compass, one of the tribesmen told Wyatt the origin of their hairy visitor.

The tribesman took Wyatt to a high rock pinnacle and told Wyatt that men came down from the sky in "a small moon" and dropped off several hairy creatures on the Earth.

Artist Neil Riebe's version of a Crazy Bear.

He also said that men from the small moon looked like normal human beings, but they had short hair and wore tight-fitting, silver clothing. According to the tribesman, the men even waved to the tribe in a friendly manner before closing the door to their spaceship and flying away!

After the "Crazy Bears" were dropped off, the tribe would round them up and escort them through their village. The natives at the time believed that the Crazy Bears were capable of "powerful medicine," which is why they fed and cared for them in the nearby caves. The tribesman apparently never told Wyatt what happened to all the other Crazy Bears that had been dropped off in the past, as he only saw one such creature during his time with the tribe.

Why would aliens drop off these Bigfoot creatures on the earth? Wyatt's grandson, James Wyatt, told paranormal investigator Brad Steiger that the aliens may have been conducting some sort of experiment.

The story of the Crazy Bears is not the only tale to associate Bigfoot with

UFOs. Many other Bigfoot sightings have occurred at the same places and times that UFOs were spotted. Some witnesses have even claimed to have seen a Bigfoot creature vanish into thin air, as if it had stepped into another dimension. Perhaps this is why a Bigfoot has never been captured in the wild.

If the story told in Wyatt's diary is true, then perhaps Bigfoot really does come from outer space. In any case, the Crazy Bear story is one of the Old West's most interesting tales concerning UFOs and mysterious creatures.

Charles Fort.

CHAPTER 5
THE CRAWFORDSVILLE MONSTER

Back in the 1800s there weren't really any serious UFO researchers like we have today. One of the first persons to begin seriously gathering together stories about strange creatures and unidentified flying objects was Charles Fort.

Born in 1874, Fort began at an early age collecting old newspaper articles, specifically anything that seemed too strange to be true. Fort eventually published the stories and his comments on them in several books. As a result, people began to refer to unexplained happenings as "Fortean events." In similar manner, strange creatures are often called Fortean monsters. In other words, monsters that are a lot stranger in appearance than Bigfoot or the dinosaur-like Loch Ness Monster.

One such Fortean monster believed to possibly be from outer space was the flying monster of Crawfordsville, Indiana, seen on September 5, 1891. Fort read about the beast in the September 10th edition of the *Brooklyn Eagle*. He was so confused by the creature's odd appearance that he figured it was a hoax. To see if this was the case or not, Fort wrote a letter to one of the eyewitnesses mentioned in the newspaper. To Fort's surprise, the man, Reverend George W. Switzer, replied to him and told him that it really happened!

It was midnight on Saturday, September 5, 1891, and Switzer had gotten up to get some water from his well when he saw what was surely the strangest sight of his life.

Snaking through the air was an almost formless creature comprised of hundreds of white fluttering fins. Reverend Switzer awakened his wife who also got to see the creature. They both said it was, "[swimming] through the air in a writhing, twisting manner similar to the glide of some serpents."

At one point the couple described the monster as swooping so close to the ground that it nearly touched the yard of a nearby home before it continued its flight over the town.

The reverend and his wife weren't the only ones to see the monster that night. So did two ice delivery men, Marshall McIntyre and Bill Gray, who had gotten up early to prepare their delivery wagon for their rounds later in the morning. Their sighting was actually the first one to be published in the local paper, having appeared on Saturday, September 5. It was about 2 a.m. on Saturday as the two were preparing the ice delivery wagon, when all of a sudden, a feeling of "awe and dread" overcame them.

Turning their heads to the sky, they saw a monster that they described as, "about eighteen feet long and eight feet wide and moved rapidly through the air by means of several pairs of side fins...

Jared Olive's depiction of the sighting.

It was pure white and had no definite shape or form, resembling somewhat a great white shroud fitted with propelling fins. There was no tail or head visible but there was one great flaming eye, and a sort of a wheezing plaintive sound was emitted from a mouth which was invisible. It flapped like a flag in the winds as it came on and frequently gave a great squirm as though suffering unutterable agony."

The two men, who said the monster hovered about three to four hundred feet in the air above them, were able to observe the creature for a whole hour. Eventually the two got scared, harnessed their horses, and left the area.

Several paranormal researchers, including Jerome Clark, have written that on the night after the first sighting, about 100 local townspeople in Crawfordsville went out late at night hoping to see the creature again and actually did. The monster flew over them and at one point flew so low that they could feel its hot breath.

Neil Riebe's rendition of the monster.

SPACE MONSTERS OF THE OLD WEST

The September 12th edition of the *Crawfordsville Weekly Journal* noted that letters were coming in from all over asking about the strange monster sighting. "Postmaster Bonnell is receiving letters every mail from people all over the country anxiously inquiring about the 'spook' which was seen here last Friday night."

So just what was this flying monster? Many paranormal researchers today think it was an "atmospheric beast" -- a sort of gaseous living organism. Famous scientist Carl Sagan even speculated such creatures could exist on gas planets like Jupiter.

A Fortean investigator living in Crawfordsville, Vincent P. Gaddis, has done more research on the monster than anyone. Gaddis said that, "All the reports refer to this object as a living thing -- in other words, one of the hypothetical atmospheric life forms that would figure in early theories about unidentified flying objects."

However, there could be a more down-to-earth, less exciting explanation for the monster. Shortly after the sightings ended, two Crawfordsville men came forward and told the local newspaper that they followed the monster as it drifted out of town. Eventually, they were able to see that the so-called "monster" was merely a huge flock of birds known as "killdeers." The two men, John Hornbeck and Abe Hernley, said the birds' many wings accounted for the "fins" of the monster, and their collective shrieking accounted for the mysterious noise. The *Crawfordsville Journal* further speculated that low visibility in the damp night air caused the misidentification and that newly installed electric lights in the town caused the birds to become frenzied.

While it's tempting to shout, "Case closed!" one must remember that while the bird explanation sounds somewhat plausible, it does not explain one important feature of the Crawfordsville monster -- the large, single, flaming eye! And all the witnesses claimed to have seen that single, horrific eye...

CHAPTER 6
ATTACK OF THE WATER BABIES

Though the name may not sound very scary, if you live near the waters of Pyramid Lake, Nevada, you should take special care around the water's edge. Because, according to legend, there are strange beings living under the water there. Beings called "Water Babies" that come out and abduct children playing near the shores.

Now, on the surface that might sound like a tale told to frighten children from playing at the water's edge. But, there's something very interesting about these so-called Water Babies. The creatures get their name from their appearance.

People claimed that they were little people with big heads and big eyes. If that sounds familiar, that is how most alien abduction victims describe the aliens who captured them.

Pyramid Lake was the home to three different but related groups of Native Americans: the Northern Paiute, the Owens Valley Paiute, and the Southern Paiute. It is called Pyramid Lake due to a rock formation that sticks out of the water and resembles a pyramid.

The Paiute Native American tribe spoke of two races of beings that lived under the waters of Pyramid Lake. The first was a race of mermaid beings ["merbeings"], and the second was a group of small, child-like creatures they called the "Water Babies."

In ancient fairy lore, beings like these "Water Babies" appeared often. Students of fairy legends, which are often eerily similar to UFO stories of alien abduction, think that the water babies appeared in disguise as human children as a way of luring children into the water. Like many E.T. encounters, the Water Babies were said to come out only at night.

SPACE MONSTERS OF THE OLD WEST

Pyramid Lake, Nevada.
Copyright by Andrew, Released under CC BY-ND 2.0
(https://creativecommons.org/licenses/by-nd/2.0/)

The book *The Desert Lake, the Story of Nevada's Pyramid Lake* contains a letter referring to the Water Babies. It was written by what was then called an "Agent of Indian Affairs," or a military officer who oversaw Native American tribes for the U.S. government. The letter was written in 1870, and stated, "The Indians had superstitious ideas about Pyramid Island. They say that their great grandfathers and grandmothers told them about seeing small 'Indians' that would appear to them at night. Their description of them was a large head and body and short legs, small feet. They believe this but none of them have ever seen it..."

There seems to be a strange connection between these small beings and aliens due to the unusually large heads. Those aliens, by the way, are called the "Greys" because of their grey skin. However, these frightening "water babies" also displayed behavior similar to another race of aliens known as the Reptilians. The Reptilians resembled humans with scales and reptile-like faces. They are also rumored to have

SPACE MONSTERS OF THE OLD WEST

A not so scary painting depicting the mythical water babies by Charles Kingsley.

the ability to shapeshift into a human disguise.

The Paiute have a legend considered to be the origin story of the so-called Water Babies. One day, near the lake shore, a woman had placed her baby on the ground as she went off to gather wood. A serpent-like creature slithered from the lake, and then swallowed the baby whole! It then disguised itself as the baby. When the mother returned and picked up what she thought was her baby, it also gobbled her up!

The fear of the Water Babies has even extended into our modern times. According to David Weatherly's 2019 book, *Silver State Monsters: Cryptids & Legends of Nevada*, the author knew a reporter for a Nevada newspaper who knew a Paiute woman. The reporter asked the woman why she had built her home so far away from the shores of the beautiful Pyramid Lake. She responded, in all seriousness, that she wouldn't dare live near the lake for fear that the Water Babies would abduct her children...

CHAPTER 7
FLYING MECHANICAL SERPENT

Back in the 1800s, the term UFO had not yet been invented. Because of that, you'll never see the term UFO in a sighting of something strange in the skies back then. Whenever a witness would see something strange in the air, they would often describe it as a meteor that was moving through the sky in an odd manner.

In 1873 came a sighting of an elongated, almost snake-like UFO. Because of that, witnesses described what they saw as a flying serpent rather than a UFO.

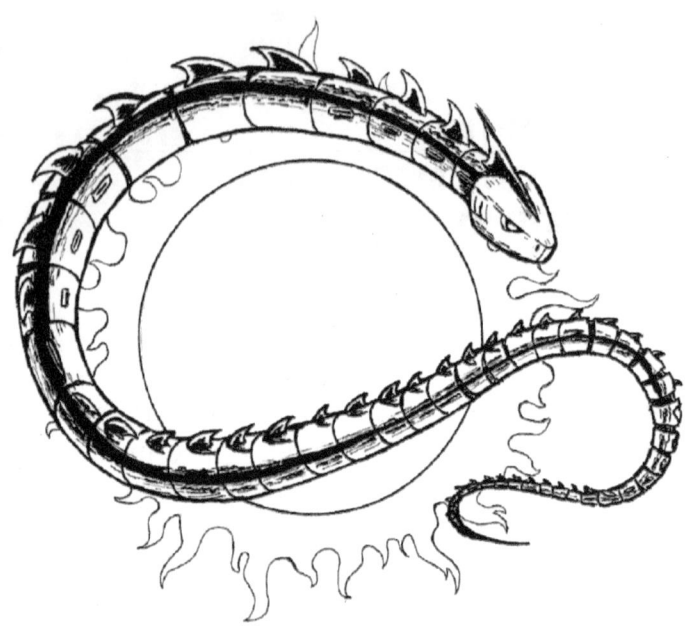

Artist Neil Riebe's rendering of the "Serpent Encircling the Sun."

SPACE MONSTERS OF THE OLD WEST

At sunrise on June 26, 1873, residents of Fort Scott, Kansas, reported seeing what looked like a "huge serpent" circling around the sun. They saw the object when the sun was about halfway above the horizon. It remained visible "for some moments."

The incident was printed in the local newspaper, the *Fort Scott Monitor*, on the following day, June 27. According to the newspaper, the sighting was reported by two very reliable witnesses. The witnesses were willing to sign sworn statements that they actually saw the flying serpent. The strange craft was reportedly also seen by several soldiers of the U.S. Cavalry, who were stationed in Fort Scott.

Additionally, a few days earlier, something very similar was seen by a farmer named Mr. Hardin, who lived a few miles east of Bonham, Texas. A serpent-like object appeared in the sky above where Hardin was working. It was also seen by several other workers standing in nearby fields. What they saw was unusual indeed, and the farmers became "seriously frightened," according to the local newspaper.

Flying serpents were a common myth across the world, such as this depiction of Quetzalcoatl from Mesoamerica.

They described what they saw as an "enormous serpent" that seemed to float upon a cloud. "It seemed to be as large and as long as a telegraph pole, was of a yellow striped color, and seemed to float along without effort," the newspaper reported.

As the farmers continued to watch, the giant snake seemed to drift off toward the east. As it moved along in the sky, the serpent behaved just like a real snake. It would coil itself up, turn over, and thrust its head forward like a snake when it is about to bite. The witnesses stated that the flying snake would "thrust forward its huge head as if striking at something, displaying the maneuvers of a genuine snake."

Years before the 1873 sightings, back in 1857 and 1858, settlers in Nebraska claimed to have also seen a huge flying serpent. Historian Mari Sandoz said that the creature was seen hovering in the sky over a steamboat. The serpent, which appeared to be "wavy," slipped in and out of the clouds. It also seemed to breathe fire and had streaks of light coming out of its sides.

SINGULAR PHENOMENON.

The Sun Encircled by a Serpent.

A strange and remarkable phenomenon was observed at sunrise yesterday morning. The sky was clear, and the sun rose entirely unobscured. When the disk of the sun was about half way above the horizon, the form of a huge serpent, apparently perfect in form, was plainly seen encircling it, and was visible for some moments. We have this statement from two reliable parties who witnessed the phenomenon, and are willing, if necessary, to make affidavit of their assertions. We have too great respect for the sun to rise before it, and therefore are innocent of the authorship of this "sea serpent" of the sun; but we have all confidence in the credibility of our witnesses. What fearful portent is indicated in this wonderful and ominous phenomenon? We shall join a Sunday school and await the solution.

Original article from the *Fort Scott Monitor*.

SPACE MONSTERS OF THE OLD WEST

The sighting in Nebraska was later put in a folksong. The song went that the serpent was a "flyin' engine/ Without no wing or wheel / It came a-roarin' in the sky / With lights along the side / And scales like a serpent's hide." To some people, this sounds more like an alien craft than a living creature.

In his book *The Flying Saucers Are Real*, Donald Keyhoe was one of the first researchers to argue that the sky serpent over Bonham was really a space craft. In the years since then, many other UFO researchers have come to agree with him.

Depiction of Spring-Heeled Jack.

CHAPTER 8
SPRING-HEELED JACK COMES TO AMERICA

Back in the 1830s, a strange entity terrorized parts of London, England. The being was humanoid in shape, but could leap vast distances impossible for normal humans. Because of this, they called him "Spring-Heeled Jack" (as though he had a spring in his shoe). Another strange detail of this man-thing was that it had a lamp attached to its chest. It was violent, and would attack women by ripping at their clothes. And the strangest details of all: it shot out blue fire and had metallic claws for hands.

Spring-Heeled Jack.

SPACE MONSTERS OF THE OLD WEST

Considering the being's strange appearance, many argued that Spring-Heeled Jack wasn't even human. Many years later, in the 1950s, UFO researcher Phil Rife was the first to speculate that Spring-Heeled Jack was really an alien.

Though Spring-Heeled Jack was never associated with UFOs during the 1830s sightings in London, in July of 1880 a similar being popped up in Louisville, Kentucky. The mysterious figure was tall and thin; wore a jumpsuit and helmet; and had a lamp on his chest. He was capable of leaping incredibly high into the air and was reported to have jumped entirely over a horse-drawn carriage and also over a haystack. In the process of jumping around and scaring people, the creature was occasionally known to grab and rip at women's clothing.

According to the web site *StrangeHistory.org*: "...women in Louisville, Kentucky began to report that they had been attacked by a man-like creature wearing black, tight clothing and a cape. He could jump great heights and distances. The attacker had long pointed fingers, ears and nose and would spit a blue glowing flame...."

In addition to the man-thing resembling Spring-Heeled Jack, there were two UFO sightings reported in newspapers that same month. On Thursday, July 29, 1880, the *Louisville Courier-Journal* reported the first of two very strange UFO incidents that could possibly have been related to the humanoid sightings.

The article, "A Flying Machine," not only included a description of the UFO, but also of the strange "man" that could be seen piloting it! The article said that witnesses saw "an object high up in the air" hovering over the Ohio River Bridge. At first the men thought it was merely a toy balloon. But, as it got closer they could see that it was clear, like glass, and that inside of it was "a man surrounded by machinery, which he seemed to be working with his feet and hands."

Even though the witnesses couldn't really describe the man within the sphere, it seems too much of a coincidence that the sphere showed up around the same time as the mysterious jumping humanoid. As for the craft itself, it sounded a bit like an autogyro, a relatively small helicopter-like craft that wasn't invented until 50 years later.

The article said that the mysterious pilot "worked his feet as though he was running a treadle," which was a mechanism activated by a foot pedal on old sewing machines. The article said that the man's arms seemed to be "swinging to and fro above his head, though the latter movement sometimes appeared to be executed with wings or fans." The mention of wings is interesting, because Spring-Heeled Jack was occasionally described as having wings too in some sightings.

Only an hour or two later, a second sighting was recorded in Madisonville, Kentucky. Then, a few weeks later, another strange being was sighted flying over New York. However, this time the being did so without the spaceship. He was seen flying with wings attached to his body. His legs were said to be like a frog's legs.

An article in the *New York Times* on September 12, 1880, reported that, "One day last week, a marvelous apparition was seen near Coney Island. At the height of at least a thousand feet in the air a strange object was in the act of flying toward the New Jersey coast. It was apparently a man with bat's wings and improved frog's legs. The face of the man could be distinctly seen, and it wore a cruel and determined expression."

The article went on to report that a similar sight had been seen several weeks prior in both Kentucky and in St. Louis, Missouri.

Actually, this wasn't the first time that a being similar to Spring-Heeled Jack had been sighted in North America. During the Civil War on the battlefield of Gettysburg, Pennsylvania, in July of 1863 was seen a strange "Spring-Heeled" being "flittering" around the dead. The man-thing was described as being tall with glowing green eyes and wearing a dark cape or cloak of some kind.

Furthermore, 1880 wasn't the last time Spring-Heeled Jack was seen in

America. In May of 1905 the jumping humanoid came to Philadelphia, Pennsylvania. A woman named Julia McGlone was leaving work when a figure leapt down and attacked her with sharp claws. The woman screamed, drawing the attention of a policeman who ran to her rescue. In the "Spring-Heeled Jack" tradition, the creature blew blue flames at the man's face and then jumped up a flight of stairs in a single bound! The strange being was wearing metallic looking clothing...

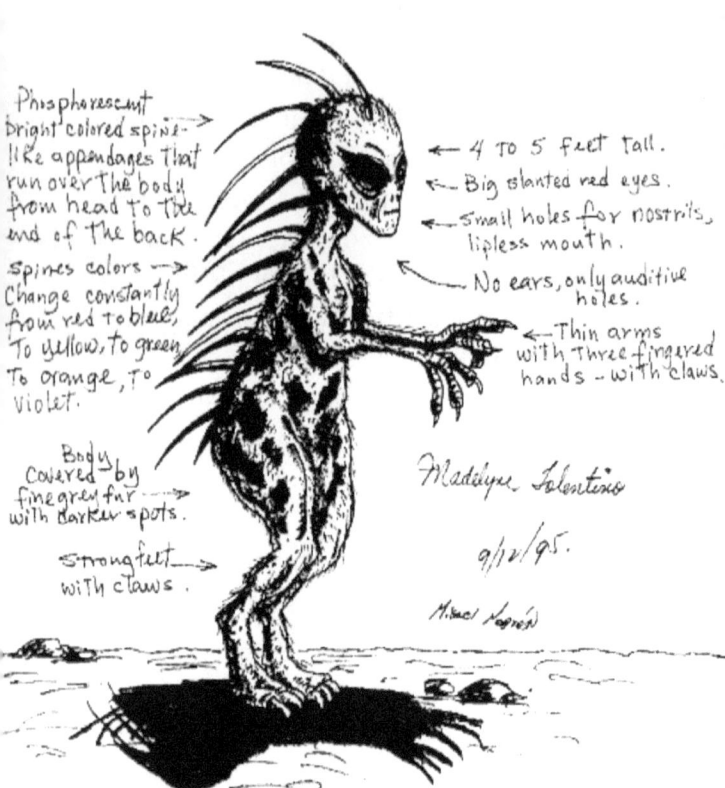

Sketch of Chupacabra allegedly seen in 1995.

CHAPTER 9
OLD WEST CHUPACABRAS

Over the years, UFOs have been associated with the appearance of certain strange creatures like Bigfoot. Another mystery animal thought to be linked to aliens is the Chupacabra.

Descriptions of the animal vary. A dramatic sighting of the creature in Puerto Rico in 1995 described it as looking similar to a Grey alien. Only this Grey had spikes that glowed in the dark. It was covered in fur, and the large eyes were red rather than black. Whether the creature was real or not, many animals in Puerto Rico were found dead, drained of all blood, in the area. The favorite animal of the bunch for the beast to attack seemed to be goats. And that is where the Chupacabra gets its name, because in Spanish it literally means "goat sucker."

Another reason the Chupacabra is associated with aliens is due to cattle mutilations. In the 1970s, cattle were often found dead mysteriously on ranches. They usually looked like they had surgery performed on them by a higher intelligence. Often times they were found drained of blood.

More recent sightings of Chupacabras make the creatures out to be more dog-like rather than alien. Cases of strange, dog-like animals that attacked cattle and drained them of all blood also occurred during the pioneer period of the Old West.

For several years Kentucky residents were terrorized by a creature that they dubbed the "dog eater." The reign of terror began in 1885 and continued off and on until the 1890s. Like so many monsters before it, the "dog eater" was given several different descriptions. Some witnesses couldn't decide whether it looked more like a panther, a big dog, or even a bear. A consistent behavior the beast had was to tear off the heads of animals and leave the bodies behind. However, occasionally it would drain the blood of its prey without eating the body.

In July of 1891 a man named G.R. Williams found a pack of dogs that he owned all dead. Upon examining their bodies, he found two puncture wounds on each neck, and each body was completely drained of blood!

Strangely, the article reported that, "There was very little evidence of a struggle, and for quite a while Mr. Williams could form no idea of the manner in which his dogs met their death."

At first, woodsmen thought perhaps it could be a panther, but all of them noted that no panther would leave behind the body. It would eat it, not drain it of blood. Clearly, they were dealing with a new animal unknown to them. The only animals they knew of to suck blood were mosquitos and vampire bats, and none of them were big enough to subdue a whole pack of dogs.

THAT MOST WONDERFUL ANIMAL.

Depiction of the "Dog Eater" from a different article.

SPACE MONSTERS OF THE OLD WEST

To catch the mystery creature, a group of hunters set out some livestock as bait and waited for the animal to show. The article said, "Just as the sentries were about to give up, however, a whine was heard, and they looked in the direction of the imprisoned cur, and the sight that met their gaze almost froze the blood in their veins."

The moon shone brightly on the form of "an immense white animal, unlike any other they had ever seen." They said it resembled a greyhound in some ways, but was bigger at four feet high and six feet long.

The men were so stunned by what they saw they forgot to fire a single bullet, and instead watched as it fed on the poor animal set out as bait. "So interested and frightened were they that not a gun was fired, and after the strange beast had finished its meal it calmly galloped away. The men went to the dead dog and found that it had been wounded in the same way as the hounds killed two nights before."

In 1896, another strange, dog-like animal comparable to today's

Chupacabras was sighted, again in Kentucky in the vicinity of Lexington. On June 17, 1896, an article appeared in the *Morning News* reporting that a Chupacabra-type creature was stalking the woods around the hamlet of Hightower, located south of Lexington.

The story said, "For the past three days, the people of Hightower, a hamlet near here, have been greatly excited over the appearance in their fields and forests of a peculiar looking, hairless animal, of a different species from any ever seen in that part of the country."

Pioneers who had lived on the land for some time often became very familiar with the animals that lived there. So if an animal seemed strange or unknown to them it probably was. They described the creature as being as tall as "a month-old calf," and said that it was fast like a fox. Its skin was pink, and the body had no hair whatsoever.

The newspaper article doesn't say anything about the creature attacking or killing livestock. However, an armed group of men pursued the animal so they must have thought it was a threat.

Furthermore, the strange animal caused people to panic. The paper wrote that, "Women, grouped together, are discussing the probability of its being a supernatural vision, appearing in advance of some dread calamity, but men are out in posses with firearms, searching the wooded sections with the purpose of solving the mystery."

And just what was this mystery beast? We may never know, but scientists and UFO researchers both are becoming doubtful that Chupacabras have anything to do with UFOs. More recently scientists have argued that the Chupacabra is most likely just a species of dog or coyote that has a disease that causes its hair to fall out!

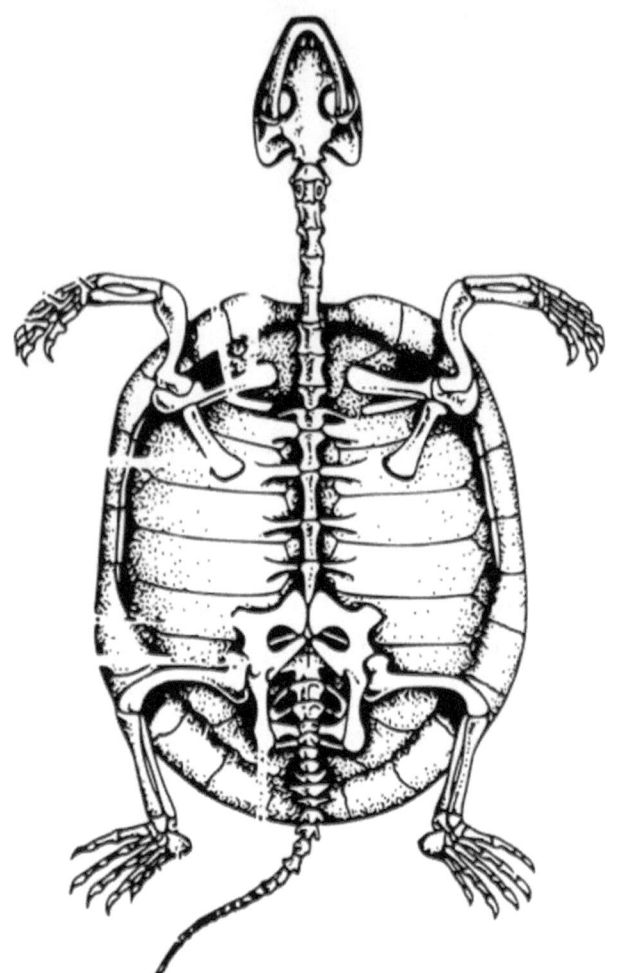

19th Century illustration of a turtle's skeleton.

CHAPTER 10
THE FLYING TURTLE UFO MONSTER

Back in the 1960s, one of the more famous movie monsters from Japan was Gamera, a giant flying turtle that breathed fire. When Gamera wanted to fly, he would pull his head, arms and legs into his shell. Jet fire would then shoot from the holes and he would begin to spin and fly just like a flying saucer. Strangely enough, in real life, something similar to Gamera was seen in the year 1813 in Portsmouth, Virginia! Stranger yet, the sighting was reported to none other than former President Thomas Jefferson!

The original letter from Hansforth to
Thomas Jefferson.

SPACE MONSTERS OF THE OLD WEST

The man who saw the fiery, turtle-like UFO was named Edward Hansforth, and was described as "a respected citizen." He had even been the harbormaster for the District of Norfolk and Portsmouth in 1802.

On July 25, 1813, Hansforth and a friend, John L. Clark of Baltimore, saw what we would today call a UFO in the skies of Virginia. It was so strange that Hansforth wrote a letter about it to Jefferson, who was then a part of an organization called the American Philosophical Society (who sometimes investigated strange things). The letter is today preserved among The Thomas Jefferson Papers Series at the Library of Congress.

At first, what Hansforth saw looked like "a ball of fire fully as large as the sun." The ball of fire was producing a lot of smoke, which sometimes made it hard to see. And this is where the story got weird. Hansford said that suddenly the strange object began to look like a turtle coming out of its shell!

It's hard to know what Hansforth meant to say for sure, but we think he meant the object at first looked like a turtle shell. After a bit, things resembling arms and legs began to come out of the shell. Whatever the case, many UFO witnesses over the years have described spacecraft as looking like shells, though none have ever acted as though they saw a flying turtle!

And still, the story got stranger as Hansforth's UFO continued to change shape. Hansforth wrote in his letter that the object "then formed the shape of a human skeleton." How it went from a turtle to a human skeleton is truly puzzling. Regardless of how this happened, after the transformation occurred, the object began to rise high in the sky and then come back down over and over again. After a while, the mysterious thing then "disappeared within its own smoke."

Considering that this object seemed to move and transform, perhaps it wasn't a space craft but was a living being of some kind. Perhaps it was an atmospheric beast similar to the Crawfordsville Monster? We will likely never know.

CHAPTER 11
THE INVISIBLE AEROLITE MONSTER

On May 30, 1869, a truly indescribable monster set foot in Ellington, Connecticut. It was indescribable because it was invisible. An article in the *Hartford Daily Courant* reported how a "brilliant aerolite" was seen over the village late one night. Aerolite was a fancy term back then for meteor. And back then, before the term UFO had been invented, many people described strange things in the sky as meteorites because they had no other term for them. But what passed over Ellington that night was no mere meteor.

After the passing of the meteor, witnesses claimed to hear "unusual sounds" coming from the center of the town. And then it happened. Suddenly, a wagon began to move under its own power into the middle of the street. Then, an unseen force tipped it upside down!

The paper wrote, "The mysterious force then moved in the direction of Deacon Smith's house and hurled one of his gates across the street, while another was carried along in a south westerly direction and dropped in front of his brother's store." Then the invisible thing, whatever it was, moved onto another wagon turning it over like it had the first.

As it continued down the road, it caused even more destruction, "upsetting a wagon of Mr. Hall's, throwing open his stable door and letting his horse loose, ringing his door bell"!

More "unusual sounds" were heard. "The next manifestation was at or near a building occupied as a wagon shop by a Mr. King but no damage was done here, and there was no special manifestation of force, but still the mysterious sounds were heard."

According to the paper, some witnesses claimed to see something causing the mayhem. They described them as "four impalpable forms of men passing and re-passing, silently as if walking in the air, in the direction of the sounds at different points." Impalpable can mean several different things, but what the paper was trying to imply was that the beings looked see-through, or transparent. In other words, they were like ghosts.

As for more strange details, witnesses also claimed to see a small, ghostly looking dog with the men! (Was it a Chupacabra after all?) The reporter covering the story said that since he did not believe in ghosts himself, he believed the excited witnesses just thought they saw the ghostly forms in the middle of all the commotion. And, interestingly, the reporter didn't imply that the story was fake. By all accounts he seemed to vouch that all the mysterious mayhem happened, he just didn't believe that the witnesses saw any ghosts.

Of course, we don't know for sure what really happened that night in Ellington. And, the meteor could have just been a coincidence. Or maybe, just maybe, the meteor was really a spacecraft containing mischievous, invisible aliens...

CHAPTER 12
THE ALIEN SUBMARINE MONSTER

By now you know what a UFO is, but have you ever heard the term USO? It stands for unidentified submersible object, which is basically a UFO seen in or under the water! Though USO sightings don't get as much attention in the media as UFOs do, they are still fairly common. Often times they are a bright light seen moving under the water like a submarine. And, believe it or not, there were USO sightings in the Old West. Only this one is surely one of the strangest USOs ever observed...

Artist's conception by Neil Riebe.

SPACE MONSTERS OF THE OLD WEST

The odd encounter occurred near Tacoma, Washington, on July 2, 1893. The story began on a Saturday afternoon (July 1) at about 4:30 when a group of "well-known gentlemen" departed Tacoma on a boat called the *Marion* for a three-day fishing and hunting trip.

After several hours of fishing on the Puget Sound, the men decided to go ashore at a place called Black Fish Bay on Henderson Island, where they would camp and spend the night. As it turned out, they made camp within 100 yards of a group of men who were engaged in surveying the area.

Sometime after midnight, one of the fishermen was awakened by a loud noise. The air was filled with "a strong current of electricity that caused every nerve in the body to sting with pain," the paper quoted one of the men as saying. He also described a bright flashing light. Because of the loud noise and electric charge in the air, the witness thought that the fishermen were caught in the middle of an intense thunderstorm. But, looking up at the sky, he saw no evidence of lightning and instead, he noticed strange lights coming from the water of the nearby bay.

By now, the other fishermen and the surveyors were awake and could also see the disturbance occurring in the water. Approaching the shore towards the frightened group was what the witness later described as "a most horrible-looking monster."

The "monster fish," as they called it, was 150 feet long, but the description sounds more like a giant caterpillar than a fish. The beast had a head that resembled a walrus, but with six eyes the "size of dinner plates."

The witness also said, "At intervals of about every eight feet from its head to its tail a substance that had the appearance of a copper band encircled its body, and it was from these many bands that the powerful electric current appeared to come."

The bizarre creature also had two horn-like protrusions sticking from its head. Since the beast was caterpillar-like, perhaps they were antennae? Even stranger, these two "horns" were spraying water that looked like "blue fire" because of its electric charge.

When one of the men approached the water, the monster seemed to become agitated and quickened its speed. This caused water to splash on the man and he fell down as though he had died!

A second man rushed to help him but he too was hit by the water and fell to the ground. The other men then ran to hide in the woods. Even from inside the protection of the trees, the men said they could see the monster's glow light up the sky, and its thunderous roar could be heard for miles around. Luckily for them, the monster never came ashore and instead changed course diving underneath the water. Although it was no longer on the surface, the men could still see the monster's glow as it traveled under the water. Eventually, its glow faded away, and the monster was never seen again.

The men made their way back to their fallen companions. Luckily, the two men were not dead, just knocked unconscious by the mysterious water.

Sketch of the monster by Jared Olive.

SPACE MONSTERS OF THE OLD WEST

Rather than a flesh and blood monster, some paranormal researchers think it was really an advanced submarine. One of the main reasons why was this odd description of the creature's tail: "Its tail from what I could see of it was shaped like a propeller, and seemed to revolve, and it may be possible that the strange monster pushes himself through the water by means of this propeller like tail."

The strange electric current in the air was another hint that it may have been a machine. The copper wire encircling the body also implied it was really a machine. And the six eyes? Maybe they were really windows or portholes for the pilots to look out of?

As was the case with many Old West UFO sightings, the objects were often described using the characteristics of known animals, such as birds, fish, and insects. In this case, the strange object seemed to be in the shape of an animal, but it may well have been a mechanical device.

Illustration from
20,000 Leagues Under the Sea.

SPACE MONSTERS OF THE OLD WEST

Although it remains a very intriguing account from the Old West, critics say that perhaps the witness made up the story for the amusement of their friends. Or if not the witnesses, then perhaps the reporter himself. Maddeningly for researchers, this was indeed an era rife with fake news stories.

Interestingly, the famous Jules Verne novel, *Twenty Thousand Leagues under the Sea*, was published in French in 1869 and in English in 1873. The novel is about an eccentric inventor who builds the world's first submarine. To the sailors who see it, the vessel appears to be a huge sea monster.

So was the Tacoma USO a real mechanical monster, or was it a hoax inspired by science fiction like *20,000 Leagues Under the Sea*? Regardless of whether it is true or not, the story remains the 19th century's most fascinating account of an underwater submersible object.

Lewis and Clark with Sacagawea.

CHAPTER 13
ALIENS WITH BOWS AND ARROWS?

In 1803 occurred the Louisiana Purchase. During that time, the U.S. government bought a great deal of land west of the Mississippi River from France. To explore this new land, Thomas Jefferson sent out the now famous exploring duo of Lewis and Clark to see what kind of secrets this new land held. Jefferson even instructed the explorers to be on the lookout for mammoths, just in case a few survived extinction in that area. Lewis and Clark found no mammoths, but they may have found reports of aliens!

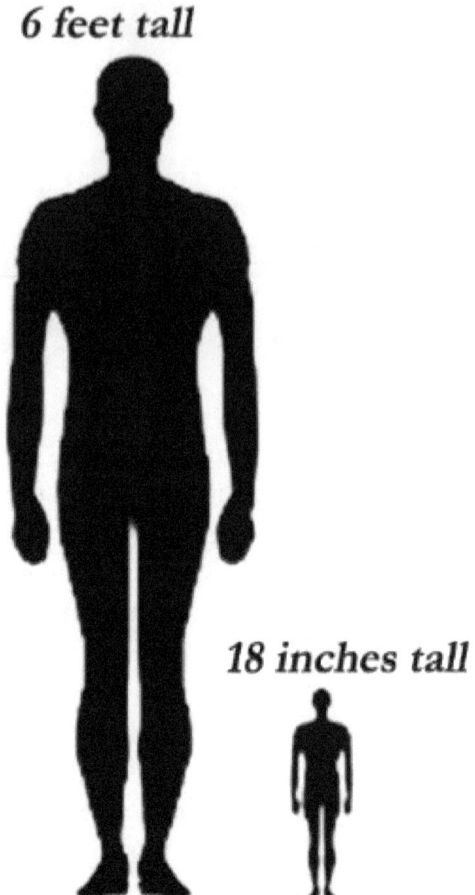

The Little People's height compared to a 6' Man.

SPACE MONSTERS OF THE OLD WEST

In August 1804 Lewis and Clark were exploring South Dakota. With them was a group of Wičhíyena Sioux Native Americans. While walking through the Pryor Mountains they pointed out a strange mound coming out of the ground. They said that the mound was the home of the "little people" and to be very cautious of them.

Lewis wrote in his journal that the Little People were "devils" with very large heads that stood only one and a half feet tall! Though this is somewhat shorter than the usual alien Grey, often reported as three to four feet tall, the short height of the beings coupled with their large heads has led some to think that these "devils" might have been aliens.

The Sioux told Lewis and Clark that these little men had special bows and arrows, which could shoot much, much further than their own bows and arrows could. They said that the devils killed anyone who approached their mound, which the Sioux called the "Spirit Mound."

The Sioux were so afraid of the little people that they dared not approach the mound. If you'd like to see what Clark himself wrote of the Little People, you can see for yourself below:

"Captain Lewis and I decided to visit a high hill situated in an immense plain three leagues N. 20° W. from the mouth of White Stone River. This hill appears to be of a conic form, and by all the different nations in this quarter is supposed to be a place of devils, or that they are in human form with remarkable large heads and about 18 inches tall; that they remarkably are very watchful and are armed with sharp arrows with which they can kill at a great distance; they are said to kill all persons who are so hardy as to attempt to approach the hill. They state that tradition informs them that many Indians have suffered by these little people and among others that three Omaha men fell a sacrifice to their merciless fury not many years since – so much do the Omaha, Sioux, Otoe, and other neighboring nations believe this fable that no consideration is sufficient to induce them to approach this hill."

SPACE MONSTERS OF THE OLD WEST

There is more to the legend of the Little People, as many other Native American tribes believed in them. According to legend, when 350 Lakota warriors fought the Little People they were defeated badly. Many of the Lakota died, and the ones who survived were injured for life.

Another story told of a Little Person who hunted and killed a full-grown bull elk and carried it on his shoulders! So, in addition to their strange arrows, the Little People were also very strong. The Little People were also capable of "powerful medicine," or magic, according to the Crow Tribe.

People have wondered if archeologists have ever found evidence of the Little People in the Pryor Mountains. This may surprise you, but the answer is yes. Physical remains of tiny people were found once in caves in Montana. They were described as being in the form of normal humans only much, much smaller. Unfortunately, the skeletons were lost and have yet to be found to this day...

Sketch of the Van Meter Visitor. Courtesy Van Meter Public Library.

CHAPTER 14
DINOSAURS FROM OUTER SPACE!

One of the strangest stories in this book took place in Van Meter, Iowa, in the spooky Fall months of 1903. On the night of September 29, a traveling tool salesman named Uly Griffith had just returned to Van Meter in his covered wagon. It was just after midnight when he noticed a strange, bright light atop one of the town buildings. As he watched the light, it suddenly darted onto the next roof.

The next night, around the same time, the town doctor, Dr. Alcott, was awakened by a bright light shining through his window. Dr. Alcott grabbed his gun and went outside to investigate. What he saw was unlike anything he could imagine. It stood eight feet tall and looked to be half man and half animal, with great wings like a bat. A glowing horn, the source of the bright light, grew from its head! Dr. Alcott shot the monster several times, but said that the bullets had no effect. And so, he ran back into his office with great fear.

The next night, on October 1, a night watchman at the bank also saw the monster. He too fired his gun at the thing and it left. On the ground outside, he found three toed tracks.

That same night it was seen by O.V. White, who owned the local hardware store. He saw the monster clinging to a telephone pole. When he fired his gun at the monster, it gave off a strange odor that was so powerful that it made White retreat back inside in a state of confusion.

White's gunshot attracted the attention of another town resident, Sidney Gregg, who watched the beast flap its wings and disappear.

In the very early morning hours of October 3rd, before the sun had risen, a man working at the local tile and brick factory, heard strange noises coming from a nearby mine. He looked outside and saw not one, but two of the creatures together lurking around the mine. One looked smaller than the other, he noted.

He went into town to alert the others, as the story of the strange visitors was by now known to the whole town. Several people from town accompanied him to the mine, where they too saw the monsters. They fired their guns at the creatures, and they descended into the depths of the mine. Everyone was too afraid to follow, and decided to create a barricade trapping the creatures inside.

The strange beings were never seen again, but just what where they? Naturally, local residents had their theories. The principal of the local school, a well-educated man, speculated that it might be a dinosaur. After all, pterodactyls had wings like a bat's. They also had long beaks, which could account for the "horn" that so many saw.

Illustration of the monster from the time.

SPACE MONSTERS OF THE OLD WEST

The dinosaur theory works well until one gets to the strange, alien glow the being emitted. As such, some UFO researchers have wondered if the "creatures" were really just aliens in strange suits meant to explore Earth? This could then mean that the bright lights seen by all could have been a search light built into the suit. If they were aliens, then the suits could have then protected the aliens from Earth's atmosphere, which could be harmful to them.

Van Meter has never forgotten the incident, and like Roswell, New Mexico and its UFO Festival, Van Meter today celebrates the "Van Meter Visitors" with an annual celebration each Fall.

Artist Neil Riebe's sketch of the original grave of the Aurora alien.

CHAPTER 15
THE ALIEN'S GRAVE

What if we told you that somewhere in a lonely Texas cemetery lies the body of an alien that crashed to Earth long ago? Don't believe us? Well, what if we told you that there was an official state marker that says this? Believe it or not, outside of Aurora, Texas, exists an official state marker about the Aurora Cemetery that mentions the legend. And, just in case you're not familiar with state historical markers, very few of them ever mention space aliens.

Before we delve into our story, we should explain that the years 1896 and 1897 (when this story takes place) were busy ones for UFO sightings. For those two years, many newspaper reports were published reporting on strange

Illustration of the crash by Neil Riebe.

ships seen in the sky. Only back then they didn't call them UFOs, they called them airships.

Of all the many airship stories from that era, the one from Aurora is the most famous. In a way, Aurora was the Old West version of the Roswell Incident. Like Roswell's 1947 UFO crash, a strange craft crashed near a small desert town and an alien body was discovered.

The Aurora Incident took place on Saturday, April 17, 1897 at 6 o'clock in the morning. A silver, cigar-shaped UFO was soaring over the skies of the town when it began to slow down. It seemed to be having some sort of mechanical or engine trouble. The townspeople watched in amazement as the slow-moving airship drifted over the town square, moved north toward the property of Judge J. S. Proctor, and then collided with a windmill on the judge's land. The craft "went into pieces with a terrific explosion, scattering debris over several acres of ground" and destroying the windmill, the adjacent water tank and the judge's flower garden.

Sketch of dying alien by Jared Olive.

The explosion and crash drew many spectators to Judge Proctor's land, where they found the dead body of the ship's pilot in the midst of the wreckage. Then the story got really weird. Witnesses said the pilot was not human!

The way that witnesses described the ship was also interesting. They said that it was made of "an unknown metal, resembling somewhat a mix of aluminum and silver." A witness guessed that the ship weighed "several tons."

We know all of this from a newspaper article written by Aurora resident S. E. Haydon published in the *Dallas Morning News*. Although the pilot's body was damaged severely in the crash, it was clear that "he was not an inhabitant of this world" and could have possibly been from Mars, according to another witness, Mr. T. J. Weems, an officer in the U.S. Signal Service and an "authority on astronomy." When the townspeople checked the pilot's body, they found that he was carrying papers written in an unknown language.

A Windmill Demolishes It.

Aurora, Wise Co., Tex., April 17.—(To The News.)—About 6 o'clock this morning the early risers of Aurora were astonished at the sudden appearance of the airship which has been sailing through the country.

It was traveling due north, and much nearer the earth than ever before. Evidently some of the machinery was out of order, for it was making a speed of only ten or twelve miles an hour and gradually settling toward the earth. It sailed directly over the public square, and when it reached the north part of town collided with the tower of Judge Proctor's windmill and went to pieces with a terrific explosion, scattering debris over several acres of ground, wrecking the windmill and water tank and destroying the judge's flower garden.

The pilot of the ship is supposed to have been the only one on board, and while his remains are badly disfigured, enough of the original has been picked up to show that he was not an inhabitant of this world.

Mr. T. J. Weyms, the United States signal service officer at this place and an authority on astronomy, gives it as his opinion that he was a native of the planet Mars.

Papers found on his person—evidently the record of his travels—are written in some unknown hieroglyphics, and can not be deciphered.

The ship was too badly wrecked to form any conclusion as to its construction or motive power. It was built of an unknown metal, resembling somewhat a mixture of aluminum and silver, and it must have weighed several tons.

The town is full of people to-day who are viewing the wreck and gathering specimens of the strange metal from the debris. The pilot's funeral will take place at noon to-morrow.

  E. E. HAYDON.

Actual Article from *Dallas Morning News*, 4-19-1897.

This is a very interesting detail because the Roswell Incident also had UFO debris with strange writing on it. The papers found on the Aurora alien may have been a record of the pilot's journeys "written in some unknown hieroglyphics" that could not be understood. As the story reached nearby towns, many visitors arrived to look at the crash. Haydon wrote in his article that, "The town is full of people today who are viewing the wreck and gathering specimens of the strange metal from the debris."

After the crash, the townspeople tried to find out more about how the airship was built and what made it fly. However, Haydon said that the ship was "too badly wrecked to form any conclusion as to its construction or motive power."

The Dallas Morning News article, published two days after the crash, said that the pilot's funeral would take place on April 18. Another newspaper, *The Fort Worth Register*, said, "The pilot, who was not an inhabitant of this world, was given a proper Christian burial at the Aurora Cemetery."

State Historical Marker at Aurora Cemetery (Photo by Noe Torres).

SPACE MONSTERS OF THE OLD WEST

Although some people claim the story is not true and was created by Aurora residents to boost tourism, many other people do think that a spaceship really did crash-land there. As we mentioned earlier, the Texas State Historical Commission really did place a permanent marker at the cemetery that mentions the spaceship crash. The marker says, "This site is also well-known because of the legend that a spaceship crashed nearby in 1897 and the pilot, killed in the crash, was buried here."

When the pilot was buried, a special grave marker was erected at the site. In 1973, a newspaper reporter named Bill Case, who was also a UFO researcher, saw the marker and said it had a drawing on it of a flying saucer. Case used a metal detector over the grave and became excited when it indicated that large pieces of metal were also buried there—possibly alien wreckage! When he asked permission to open the grave he was unfortunately denied.

The Aurora Monument
(2020 Photo by Daniel Alan Jones).

SPACE MONSTERS OF THE OLD WEST

Worse still, shortly after Case wrote his story on the marker, thieves stole the alien's tombstone! Because of this, the exact spot of the pilot's body became unclear over time. Today, nobody is exactly sure where the pilot was buried.

The case of the alien that fell from the sky in Aurora, Texas, continues to fascinate people to this very day. It has been featured on many television documentaries and in many books, and a number of UFO researchers, especially in North Texas, are still seeking answers to the puzzling events of 1897.

Marker in Aurora, Texas
(2020 Photo by Daniel Alan Jones).

Also Available

About the Author

Noe Torres is a recognized expert in the field of UFOs and the paranormal. He is an author, publisher, and member of the Mutual UFO Network (MUFON). He holds a Bachelor's in English and a Master's in Library Science from the University of Texas at Austin. He has written one of the most popular books about the famous Roswell Incident, titled *Ultimate Guide to the Roswell UFO Crash*, which is the top selling book among tourists visiting Roswell, New Mexico. He has also written several other well-reviewed books, including *Mexico's Roswell*, *The Other Roswell*, *Aliens in the Forest*, *Fallen Angel*, and *The Coyame Incident*.

About the Author

John LeMay was born and raised in Roswell, New Mexico, the town where aliens and a UFO allegedly crashed in 1947. He has written over twenty books on western history and folklore like this one. He is the co-author of the series *The Real Cowboys and Aliens* (about UFOs in the Old West) with Noe Torres and is also the author of the *Cowboys & Saurians* series, about dinosaur sightings from the Pioneer Period.

John LeMay (left) and Noe Torres (right) at the Roswell UFO debris field in 2012.

www.ingramcontent.com/pod-product-compliance
Lightning Source LLC
Chambersburg PA
CBHW060403080526
44583CB00012B/451